FIREFLIES IN THE DARK

The Story of
Friedl Dicker-Brandeis
and the Children of Terezin

by Susan Goldman Rubin

SCHOLASTIC INC.
New York Toronto London Auckland Sydney
Mexico City New Delhi Hong Kong

For my brother, Edwin P. Moldof

ISBN 0-439-29694-3

Text copyright © 2000 by Susan Goldman Rubin.
All rights reserved.
Published by Scholastic Inc., 555 Broadway, New York, NY 10012,
by arrangement with Holiday House, Inc.
SCHOLASTIC and associated logos are trademarks and/or registered
trademarks of Scholastic Inc.

12 11 10 9 8 7 6 5 4 3   1 2 3 4 5 6/0

Printed in the U.S.A.   14

First Scholastic printing, April 2001

Back cover: photo of Friedl Dicker-Brandeis, circa 1936

Picture Credits

The prints and photographs in this book are from the following sources and
are used with permission:

Jewish Museum in Prague: Pages 1, 2 (bottom, left and right), 4, 5, 6, 7, 9 (bottom, left
  and right), 10, 15 (left and right), 16 (bottom), 17 (top right, bottom left and right),
  18 (bottom), 19 (top and bottom), 20 (top and bottom), 21, 22, 25, 26, 30 (left and
  right), 31 (right), 32, 33, 35 (top and bottom), 38, 42 (top and bottom), 43 (top left
  and bottom right), and front cover (bottom right).
Getty Research Institute, Research Library, 920030: Page 24.
Edith Kramer: Page 8 (right).
Ela Steinová-Weissberger: Pages 9 (bottom right), 32.
Pamatnik Terezin: Pages 8 (left), 12, 13, 27, 29, 31 (left), 34, and back cover.
Courtesy of the Simon Wiesenthal Center Library and Archives: Pages 14, 18 (top),
  42 (left).
Kitty Passerová-Levy: Page 15 (left) and front cover (bottom right)
Lilly Edna Amit: Page 16 (top).
Staatliche Museum zu Berlin: Page 17 (top left).
Alfred Kantor: Page 37 (top and bottom).
Beit Theresienstadt: Pages 39, 41.
Yad Vashem Film & Photo Archives: Page 40 and front cover (center).
Helga Polláková-Kinsky: Page 44.

Title page: Flowers in a Glass *by Friedl Dicker-Brandeis*

Pencil drawing by Gertruda Eisingerová
(December 27, 1931–October 23, 1944)

Pencil drawing by Liliana Franklová
(January 12, 1931–October 19, 1944)

Acknowledgments

I want to thank the many people who helped me with this book. First, those who actually were at Terezin who told me about their experiences, allowed me to read their diaries, and loaned me precious artwork and photographs. In May 1998, I went to Prague and interviewed Dana Liebl. There I was able to attend a meeting of the Terezin Initiative, an association founded in 1989 by former prisoners who wanted to save Terezin as a memorial for future generations. There Dana introduced me to Eva Štichová-Beldová, Helga Weissová-Hošková, Kurt Jiří Kotouč, and Doris Grozdanovicová. Through Dana's efforts, I was also able to speak to Raja Englanderová-Žákníková over the phone.

At the Jewish Museum in Prague I received help from Michaela Hajková, Curator of Painting and Graphic Collection, and Dr. Anita Franková, Chief Archivist of the Archive of the Holocaust. At Terezin I met Dr. Jan Munk, Director of the Terezin Memorial.

Incredible friendships were formed in L410. Back home in California I had lunch with Dasha Lewin, Dana Liebl's best friend from L410 in Terezin. Ela Steinová-Weissberger, one of the "girls of Room 28" in L410, who now lives in Tappan, New York, talked to me over the phone. She also put me in touch with *her* best friend, Helga Polláková-Kinsky, who lives in Vienna, and with Charlotte Verešová in Prague. Finally I had the pleasure of meeting Ela in person when she came to Irvine, California, to introduce a production of *Brundibár* put on by Opera Pacific. (At Terezin Ela played the cat in *Brundibár*. Today, as one of the few surviving performers, she goes around the world introducing performances of the children's opera.) I immediately recognized Ela because I had seen her in documentary films written and directed by another survivor, Zuzana Justman.

On a trip to New York I visited Zuzana, who told me about *The Book of Alfred Kantor*. I talked with artist and art therapist Edith Kramer on the phone. Edith studied art with Friedl in Vienna, then in Prague, and assisted Friedl in her work with children. Later when Edith immigrated to the United States and became an art therapist, she based her methods on Friedl's.

Other Terezin survivors now in Israel who studied art with Friedl at Terezin are Willi Groag, the head tutor of L410, Dita Polachová-Kraus, one of Friedl's most talented students, and Lilly Edna Amit, who vividly remembered her time in L410. I spent a couple of days with Dr. Susan E. Cernyak-Spatz, a professor of Holocaust Literature and Foreign Languages at the University of North Carolina at Charlotte. Susan not only told me about Terezin and gave me English translations of unpublished diaries written by other former prisoners, she also took me to the university library and translated vital information from German on the spot.

One contact led to the next as amazing

stories kept coming my way. A long letter arrived from Gerhard Lilienfeld in Germany, telling me about Q609, the boys' home he lived in at Terezin. Through Jane Wesley, Curator of the Sydney Jewish Museum, I received a letter from Jerry Rind in Australia, who recalled how he stole lumber at Terezin to use as scenery for *Brundibár*.

Ela Steinová-Weissberger helped me track down Kitty Passerová-Levy, who also lives in Australia. It turned out that Kitty's beautiful collage, "Flowers in a Vase," done at Terezin under Friedl's guidance, is a jewel in the crown of the Sydney Jewish Museum. Prime Minister Paul Keating himself helped bring the collage to Australia.

These are the people who actually lived the events described in this book and who have encouraged me to tell a new generation of children about Terezin.

I also want to thank the following for so generously helping me research text and art: Adaire J. Klein, Director of Library & Archival Services, and Fama Mor, Archivist and Curator, Simon Wiesenthal Center and Museum of Tolerance; the entire Library and Archival Services staff of the Simon Wiesenthal Center and Museum of Tolerance; Dr. Margaret E. Crahan of Hunter College; Diane Speilman, Public Services and Development Coordinator and Renata Stein, Curator, Leo Baeck Institute in New York City; and Alexandra Zapruder.

I am especially grateful to Anita Tarsi, Director General of Beit Theresienstadt, and Alisa Shek for reviewing my manuscript for historical accuracy and answering all my questions.

Last, I owe a debt of thanks to my friend author Sonia Levitin, who escaped from the Holocaust in Germany as a young child, but whose grandmother Lucie Goldstein was imprisoned at Terezin. I also want to thank my agent, George M. Nicholson, and my editor, Mary Cash, both of whom believed in this project from the start.

Siblings *by Gabi Freiová*
(January 1, 1933–May 18, 1944)

Contents

Watercolor by Jiří Munk (April 24, 1930–October 1944)

Pencil drawing by Hana Zieglerová (May 16, 1933–   )

Introduction

Friedl Dicker-Brandeis was an artist and a teacher who worked with children through art. Kind, motherly, and courageous, she inspired hundreds of children as the threat of death hung over them in the Terezin concentration camp. Friedl sustained their hope. She prepared them for what she believed would be a return to normal life after the war ended, when she thought they would be released.

A series of historical events led to the establishment of Terezin and the imprisonment of Friedl and her students there. In 1933 Adolf Hitler became Chancellor of Germany and set up a dictatorship. He outlawed any political parties except his own, the National Socialist German Workers' Party. Its members were the Nazis. Hitler established concentration camps, where he imprisoned people who opposed him and millions of others he simply did not like. The people Hitler hated most were the Jews. He blamed them for all of Germany's troubles, even though the Jews had done nothing wrong.

Hitler and his staff planned to get rid of every single Jew in Europe. They called this plan "the final solution." To achieve this goal they first rounded up Jews and forced them to live in separate parts of the city called ghettos. Jews were not allowed out of the ghettos, which were sealed off with barbed wire or high walls. From the ghettos, the Nazis sent the Jews to concentration camps, and then to death camps, where they were murdered.

Hitler planned to conquer other countries and create a huge German empire. When his troops invaded Czechoslovakia and Poland in 1939, Britain and France declared war on Germany, and World War II began.

Friedl Dicker-Brandeis lived in Prague, Czechoslovakia, when the Nazis came to power. Although in 1938 friends arranged to get her a visa to Palestine, which is now called Israel, she refused to leave her husband and friends.

Over time the Nazis took more and more rights away from Jews. Jews lost their jobs, businesses, and homes. Children could only go to Jewish schools. All Jews, including Friedl, wore yellow stars marked *Jude,* which means "Jew" in German. Friedl was one of the unfortunate people who were eventually sent to concentration camps.

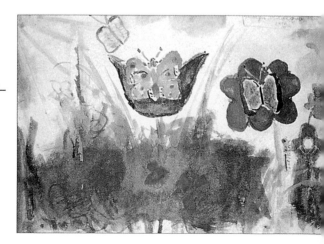

Flowers and Butterflies *by Margit Koretzová (April 8, 1933– April 1944)*

Chapter 1
Arriving at Terezin

"If we're only given a day, we have to live it."
—Friedl Dicker-Brandeis

Friedl Dicker-Brandeis received the dreaded order in 1942. She would have to leave her home and go to a concentration camp. *Concentration camp.* The very words terrified all Jews. What would happen to them in the camps? The Nazis called it "resettlement" and claimed they would treat the Jews well and give them work and food. But what if they were lying?

Not to obey a Nazi order was unthinkable. Soldiers with guns enforced the new command. Friedl knew what the Nazis were like. Once, in 1934, she had been arrested and taken to Nazi headquarters for questioning about her political activities. The experience frightened her terribly. Afterward she painted a picture of her interrogation and showed the officer questioning her baring his teeth like a ferocious animal.

Now in December 1942, Friedl, her husband, Pavel Brandeis, and all the Jews in their town of Hronov would be transported to a camp the Czechs called Terezin (called Theresienstadt by the Germans). In 1938 Friedl and Pavel had

Photo of Friedl, Prague, probably 1936. Friends said Friedl had a great sense of fun and was "always ready to joke." "She had a short haircut and big, very expressive eyes," remembered her student Raja Englanderová-Žákníková.

Portrait of Pavel Brandeis *by Edith Kramer, pencil, 1937. Edith studied with Friedl in Vienna and Prague, then became her assistant.*

already given up their large, comfortable apartment in Prague and moved to Hronov, in the country, for safety. There they lived in a storeroom on the ground floor of a house. Then in 1940 they were forced to move to a nearby store shed, and last to a small unheated attic room in another family's house. But at least those places were their homes, filled with the few things they still owned, places where friends and relatives could gather and visit despite the war.

The week before Friedl left, her best friend, Hilde Angelini-Kothny, a non-Jewish German, came to help her get ready. "I do not know how many times we packed, unpacked and repacked everything," Hilde recalled. Friedl agonized over what to bring. What would she need most? The Nazis allowed each person to take only about 110 pounds of luggage. Friedl had worked with children before and knew there would be children at Terezin. She knew they'd be lonely and terrified. She thought about how she could help them. So instead of packing things to make her own life better and more comfortable, she mainly took art supplies: paint, brushes, paper, and books—not for herself but for the children. Small but determined, she formed a plan. Through art she could fight back.

Children studying with her who were also being sent to Terezin came over to ask what kinds of art supplies they should bring. Friedl told them.

At 4 A.M. on December 16, it was time to go. Just as Friedl was about to leave, she lost her courage and burst into tears. But she was not crying for herself. She worried about what would happen to Hilde during the war. But Hilde was more worried about Friedl. No one could know what would happen.

Prisoners, guarded by a "gendarme," on the march from the Bohusovice station to Terezin.

Ghettowache by Ela Steinová-Weissberger (June 30, 1930–   ), watercolor. One of Friedl's students drew a Czech policeman.

Friedl, Pavel, and the other Jews in their town traveled by train to the city of Hradec Králové, and from there to a station near the camp. Each person had a transport number. It was printed on every piece of luggage. On December 17 Friedl, Pavel, and the others walked the last mile and three quarters to Terezin, carrying their heavy suitcases and knapsacks. Friedl was forty-four years old when she first set eyes on the prison.

At Terezin, Czech police wore their old uniforms with swastikas or Nazi symbols on their caps. They also carried guns. "March! March!" they screamed at the new prisoners arriving in groups of about a thousand at a time while German SS officials watched. *SS* stands for the German word *Schutzstaffel*; the SS were Hitler's special squads. It was their job to carry out the final solution. Terezin was an old Czech army fortress with ramparts and high brick walls, making it easy for the Nazis to turn the whole town into a ghetto/concentration camp for Jews. The Nazis had ordered the non-Jewish soldiers and residents to leave and find other homes. There was also a jail called the Little Fortress a mile away for those who did not obey the rules.

Friedl lugged her suitcase down the snowy road. Inside the camp there was terrible confusion. Thousands crowded the streets. The elderly, wearing ragged clothes, shuffled along. A cart loaded with coffins rolled by. A high wooden fence topped by barbed wire separated the ghetto population from a walkway that was to be used only by the SS. The walkway led from the headquarters of the SS to their living quarters. They didn't want to mingle with the Jews.

At the Magdeburg barracks, Friedl and her husband waited in a seemingly endless line to register. Camp police took away valuables—

Terezin Barracks *by Sonja Waldsteinová, (November 28, 1926–   ), watercolor. Sonja came to Terezin when she was sixteen, and she studied with Friedl.*

money, jewelry, and even wristwatches—from the new prisoners. They also stole whatever they wanted from the luggage. Fortunately for Friedl, nobody seemed to want her art supplies and books. She knew she would need those things to cope with whatever came.

When Friedl finally reached the head of the line and presented her identification papers, she received her work assignment. The Jewish leaders who ran the camp for the Nazis tried to give new prisoners jobs that fit their special skills. Friedl had been a painter, designer, teacher, and art therapist who had taught and cared for children. She was assigned to work with children again and to live in L410, a home for girls. All adults had to work so the children needed supervision and care. Friedl was not allowed to live with her husband. Pavel, a carpenter, was sent to a building for men.

At Terezin, all families were torn apart. Helga Weissová-Hošková, who was twelve years old when she came to Terezin from Prague with her parents, kept a diary. Her diary includes a description of her arrival at the registration building, holding on to her father's hand. She wrote in it:

They lead us inside. "Now then, men to the left, women carry on!"

"So what, I can hold my daddy's hand, can't I?"
"Hurry, hurry, did you not hear what I said?"
"Good-bye, Daddy," and the stream of people sweeps me along to the courtyard. . . .
What's going to happen? Maybe we'll never see each other again, Daddy.

But Helga's father was sent to the same barracks as Helga, a floor below hers, and she did see him again. When he was moved to another building, she smuggled drawings to him and he secretly sent letters to her. Later, she moved to Room 28 in L410. After a while, children were allowed to visit their parents on Sundays for two hours. Later, they could see them any day after work. The rules kept changing.

Parents often thought it was better for children to live together rather than with old people who were sick and dying. However, some girls, like Helga, and boys younger than twelve remained with their mothers at first. Many boys fourteen and up stayed with their fathers. The rest of the children (about half) lived together in large buildings that had once been army barracks. Each building was divided into cramped rooms that held twenty or thirty children arranged by age. Tutors like Friedl supervised the children. The places they lived in were called homes.

Chapter 2
L410, a Home for Girls

"I turned out more courageous than I had supposed."

—Friedl Dicker-Brandeis,
postcard to Hilde Kothny

At Terezin, conditions were miserable. In L410, three-tiered bunks filled unheated, overcrowded rooms. The rooms were freezing in winter and suffocatingly hot in summer. Twelve-year-old Helga Polláková-Kinsky drew a picture of the bunk beds in her diary and wrote, "We sleep, live, and eat on them. We lie next to each other on them like herrings. It's smelly, stifling, and there are fleas and bedbugs." The children missed their parents and their own familiar homes. Even under the harsh conditions of wartime when there was a shortage of food, fuel, blankets, clothing—everything—they had felt safe and comfortable in their old homes. "I wanted to go back to the family," recalled Helga. "I wasn't used to living in a bigger community of children."

Ze'ev Shek, a young man who taught Hebrew and lived in Home One of House 417, later said that he "knew that the children often woke up at night, staring into empty darkness, and sometimes heard their quiet sobs." But the teachers and caretakers could not help all the children at once. They were too busy taking care of those who were sick, giving them pills, or waking up the ones who might wet their beds and walking them to the toilet.

To keep prisoners from making friends or feeling settled, the Nazis kept moving them around. Yet wherever Friedl lived, she had a knack for creating little rooms for herself. "Friedl made a living corner in one of the corridors of L410," remembered Willi Groag, the head tutor, who knew her well. The halls had very high ceilings. Friedl cleverly made a little private place up high. One could climb a ladder to reach it. Pavel occasionally managed to see her. He built some furniture for her out of wood and bits of junk. "Later, she made a room in a small courtyard in back of L410," said Willi.

L410, formerly an army barracks, was a "home" for girls between the ages of eight and sixteen.

Karel Is Sick and Reads Aloud *by an unknown artist, collage. A piece made by one of Friedl's students shows the children's three-tiered bunks.*

Lilly Edna Amit, who lived in L410, recalled that Friedl's room in the courtyard had actually been a woodshed. Eva Štichová-Beldová described that room as "cozy" and said Friedl shared it with Irena Krausová, who taught literature. Another of Friedl's rooms was said to be in the attic of L410. But wherever Friedl shaped a place for herself, she invited the girls to visit. And they loved it.

Friedl was good at turning bare spaces into cozy places because before the war she had designed houses, apartments, and shops. She had designed places for children, including kindergartens in Vienna and Prague, and everything in them, from stackable, child-sized chairs to toothbrush holders. Friedl learned these skills at the Bauhaus, a world-famous school of modern art and crafts in Germany. Bauhaus artists studied color and experimented with materials. They produced everyday things that would make life more beautiful and comfortable. In L410 Friedl needed these skills more than ever.

Chapter 3
The Secret Schools

"Friedl. We called her Friedl. Everything was forgotten for a couple of hours. We forgot all the troubles we had."

> —Helga Polláková-Kinsky, *Voices of the Children*, documentary / videocassette

School was not allowed at Terezin. The Nazis only permitted the Jewish children to study music and crafts such as sewing, embroidering, and making pleasant, decorative pictures and greeting cards. So Friedl and the other tutors taught other subjects in secret. During lessons one of the students was posted outside as a lookout. If the ghetto guards or an SS man came along, the lookout gave a signal. Then all the students quickly hid their drawings, exercise books, and pencils and started singing or cleaning the room. Kurt Jiří Kotouč, who lived in L417, remembered that classes were "mainly held in the attics, where there was less danger that the SS would suddenly burst in on us."

Since there were no textbooks, the tutors wrote down what they knew about their subjects from memory, and they shared the books they had brought. Children fourteen and older had to work all day, so they studied at night or early in the morning, and on Sunday.

Friedl went from room to crowded room giving lessons to anyone who was interested—even to sick children in the hospital. She was small and lively. Many of the children were taller than she was. Friedl brought paper, paint, and pencils. When she ran out of materials, she used wrapping paper or the backs of blueprints and office

Portrait by an unknown artist, pencil. Subjects for art lessons included portraits and self-portraits.

Flowers in Vase by Kitty Passerová-Levy (September 4, 1929–   ), collage. Kitty made a collage by pasting colored scraps of paper on a piece of ledger paper from the office, and painting over it with tempera.

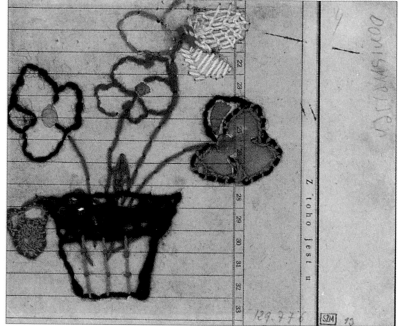

Flowers Embroidered on Office Form by Doris Weiserová (May 17, 1932–April 10, 1944) thread. Doris embroidered flowers in wool on an old office form.

forms "borrowed" from the administrative offices. According to Lilly Edna Amit, taking things from the Germans wasn't considered stealing. The prisoners called it "organizing."

Everyone waited eagerly for a turn to work with Friedl, especially the girls in Room 28. "She was cheerful, very gentle and patient," remembered Raja Englanderová-Žákníková. In Room 28 there was only one table, recalled Helga Polláková-Kinsky, so the girls drew in their bunks. Or they "squeezed somewhere and worked on their knees," said Dita Polachová-Kraus. Sometimes they went to Friedl's room.

Through art, Friedl helped the children escape mentally. "She wanted us to get away and go into a nice world," said Helga.

At the end of every lesson, Friedl's students would always sign their pictures with their names.

Sailboat *by Lilly Edna Amit (October 20, 1927–   ), watercolor. One time Friedl told the children to make something really dark, then something light. Edna may have thought of herself as the little red boat heading into a storm. The candle, moon, and stars lighting her way suggest hope.*

Color study with landscape by Josef Novák (October 25, 1931–May 18, 1944), watercolor. Sometimes the children did color studies. Josef's rainbow and the sun shining above it express his faith that life will be good again.

The Glass of Wine *by Jan Vermeer (1632–1675)*

Study by Marie Mühlsteinová (March 31, 1932–October 16, 1944)

Study by Sona Spitzová (February 17, 1931–October 6, 1944)

Study by Zweig Gustav (July 31, 1930–October 4, 1944)

The older children looked at Friedl's art books and studied paintings of the Old Masters, just as she had as a student. Then they made their own collage versions with torn strips of colored paper.

Portrait by Lea Pollak
(March 21, 1930–
May 18, 1944), pencil

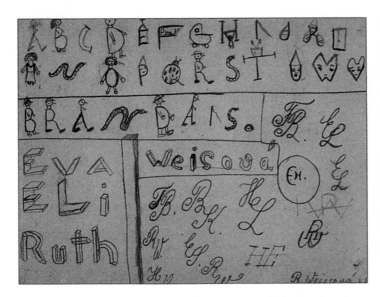

Capital Letters *by Ruth Weissová (May 17, 1932–October 4, 1944), pencil. Some lessons focused on monograms. Drawing designs of their names helped the children remember who they were. The Nazis called them by their transport numbers.*

In Friedl's classes children never used their transport numbers. Sometimes they added the numbers of their rooms and the date. Friedl would collect the pictures and store them in a cardboard box or her suitcase for safekeeping.

In the evenings, she would study the pictures as an art therapist and discuss them with other specialists. The drawings revealed the children's problems. Friedl tried to understand so that she could help. She knew the children were homesick. One child wrote this poem:

> *Ah, home, home,*
> *Why did they tear me away?*
> *Here the weak die easy as a feather*
> *And when they die, they die forever.*

Pencil drawing by Karel Sattler (November 16, 1932– May 18, 1944). Friedl always included "free lessons." That meant the children could draw anything they wanted. Some recorded the horrors they saw around them, such as prisoners taking the dead away.

Pencil drawing by Josef Novák (October 25, 1931–May 18, 1944) of an execution of a Jewish prisoner

Landscape by Robert Bondy (May 1, 1932–October 6, 1944), watercolor. Robert Bondy painted empty landscapes over and over again with his village in the distance.

Collage with Signpost: Praha *by an unknown artist. Others made pictures of signposts pointing the way back to Prague. But in this piece a dark person in a military uniform blocks the way. However, rays of sunshine break through a threatening sky, suggesting hope.*

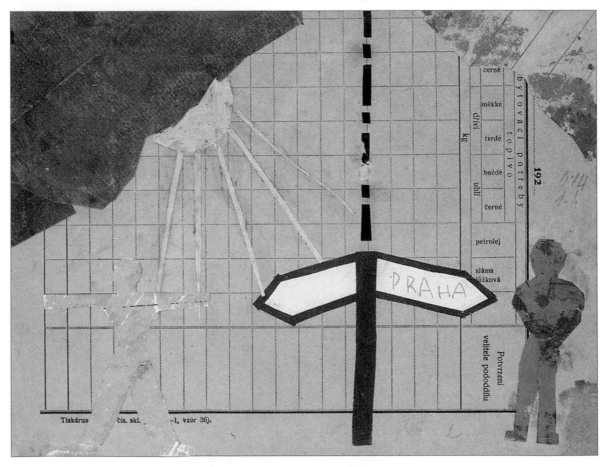

Chapter 4
Everyone Was Hungry

"We live like chained dogs."

—Jiří Zappner, *Vedem,*
underground magazine, Terezin, 1942–1944

At Terezin everyone was hungry. Old people suffered the most. They did not receive enough to eat and had to hold out their metal bowls and beg for soup. Helga Polláková-Kinsky wrote in her diary, "I went to see my uncle in the Sudeten barracks and there I saw them throw out potato peelings and ten people threw themselves on the little pile and fought for them."

Some teachers gave lessons in exchange for bread. But not Friedl. "I think Friedl was the only one who didn't take a crumb of bread for lessons," remembered Erna Furman. "She simply gave herself to us."

The Jewish leaders who ran the camp distributed better food and larger portions to the children. But there still wasn't enough, and what there was tasted terrible. Daily rations consisted of a cup of so-called coffee in the morning, at noon a disgusting watery soup that now and then

Queue for Food, *detail of drawing by Liana Franklová (January 12, 1931–October 19, 1944), pencil. Prisoners line up and wait for the cook to serve them from a vat.*

Sedez.

MEITNER EVA   skup IV. řím 11

contained a turnip, potato, or dumpling, and soup again and maybe a bun in the evening. Every three days the children received a few ounces of moldy black bread delivered in the same carts that carried corpses. They cut off the moldy parts and sliced the rest into thin pieces to make it last.

Children took care of the vegetable gardens

The Seder Supper *by Eva Meitnerová (May 1, 1931–October 28, 1944), pastel on paper. When Friedl told the children to draw memories of home, Eva did a picture of a family celebrating Passover.*

that belonged to the SS. They watered the plants, picked caterpillars off the cabbages, and occasionally succeeded in stealing a tomato or turnip. But if they were caught, they were severely punished and sent to prison in the Little Fortress.

On Sundays the children were given a pat of margarine and a teaspoonful of jam. For special occasions like Hanukkah, the girls in L410 would save up their margarine and jam and make a "bread cake" or sandwiches. "We ate it together and had our feast," recalled Helga Polláková-Kinsky.

Charlotte Verešová wrote in her diary, "I've begun to think too much about food." During Friedl's art lessons the children often drew pictures of families gathered around the dinner table, dishes heaped with food.

With so many people squeezed together it was almost impossible to keep clean. "Two toilets for 100 children aren't enough," wrote Helga. Rose Salomon shared a latrine with fifty-three other women, and described it: "When I went along the dark, rough corridor for the first time, saw the five holes side by side, and smelled the stink of chlorine and Lysol, I almost passed out."

Paula Frahm wrote, "The little piece of soap we received now and then was guarded like the greatest luxury." Children lined up in the courtyard to take turns washing at a tap with cold water. In the winter, one of the youth leaders forced his boys to wash themselves in snow. In the summer, the children showered only once a month.

There were bugs, lice, and fleas everywhere. On July 31, 1943, Helga wrote in her diary: "This is the second day I've been sleeping in the corridor because of bedbugs. There are seven of us girls sleeping outside and we've all been bitten. . . . I caught six fleas and three bedbugs today. . . . A rat slept in my shoe."

Fleas, bedbugs, and rats spread disease. Epidemics of typhoid, scarlet fever, tuberculosis, and infectious diarrhea raged through the camp. When the children got sick they were sent to the infirmary and hospital. There, Jewish doctors and nurses also imprisoned at Terezin did what they could to make their patients well with only limited supplies of medicine. Sometimes so many children were sick, there wasn't room for all of them in the infirmary.

Helga Weissová-Hošková had moved to L410 because her parents thought she would be better off living with other girls her age. She wrote in her diary, "This isn't a Home anymore, it's a regular hospital. The number of sick goes up every day. The rooms are full of patients and the doctor does not know what to do."

The Germans worried about catching the prisoners' diseases, so they shipped inmates—sick or not—to other camps "in the East." No one knew for sure what awaited them there. Rumors spread that the Nazis had built a death camp in Poland, east of Terezin, called Auschwitz-Birkenau. The fear of being sent to the East terrified everyone. The summons often came in the middle of the night. Those called up for transport had to leave in twenty-four hours. They reported to the train station, and ghetto guards crammed them into freight cars.

Friedl wrote to her friend Hilde Kothny, "If only we would not have to be afraid continuously they will send us on!"

A child wrote a poem:

How many transports? How many?
Three? Two? One? I don't know.
Our turn has come, mummy is
gathering things . . .

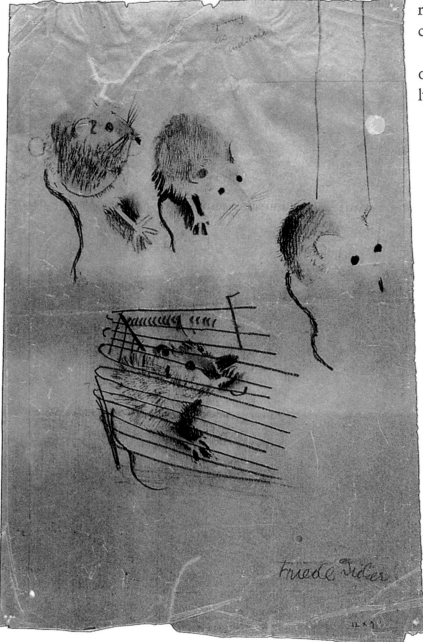

Study of Mice *by Friedl Dicker-Brandeis, pencil and charcoal drawing. Friedl used the mice as models in one of the few drawings she did at Terezin. She saved most of her art supplies for the children.*

Chapter 5
Drawing Dreams

"I feel like a bird trapped in a cage with other birds."

—The Diary of Helga Polláková-Kinsky

I was once a little child
Three years ago,
That child who longed for other worlds.
But now I am no more a child
For I have learned to hate.
I am a grown-up person now,
I have known fear.

In September 1943, transports to the East included 285 children under the age of fourteen. Friedl must have felt heartsick when she went to give drawing lessons and found some of her beloved students missing. She and the other tutors tried to protect the children. Yet there was little they could do except work with the ones who remained and keep up their strength through activities.

On Saturday, September 4, five girls in Room 28 of L410 were ordered to leave on a transport. One of them was Helga Polláková-Kinsky's best friend, Zdenka. Helga and the other girls in the room collected food and clothing in their free time for those going away.

"Saying good-bye was hard," wrote Helga. "We all cried."

That night she had nightmares. What would happen to Zdenka? No one who went to the East ever came back. "Transports, transports, that awful word terrifies the Jews of Terezin," she wrote.

Some children expressed their fear by writing poems in their free time. Hanuš Hachenburg, a teenager, wrote *Terezin:*

Other children couldn't put their feelings into words, so they used a secret code—the secret code of drawing that Friedl understood. Under her guidance they drew pictures showing what they dreaded most: transports. And to comfort themselves, they drew their dreams. Helga painted a meadow at sunset. In the world of her drawing there was no danger, no threat of transport, and while she was drawing she felt safe and good. From morning till night, in their free time, the children kept drawing. Friedl encouraged the children to talk about their artwork. Discussion helped calm them and restore their hope.

Detail from pen and ink drawing by Ruth Heinová (February 19, 1934–October 1944). Children about to leave on a transport.

A Train Travelling Through a Night Landscape *by Alice Guttamanová (September 16, 1928–September 1943), charcoal. A train hurtling through the night, carrying the prisoners into the unknown.*

At the end of the workday, the children were allowed to visit their parents and relatives for one hour. Sometimes there were longer visits on Saturday afternoons and Sundays. But there were no visits at all when the SS withdrew passes and confined the children to quarters. This happened when prisoners tried to escape or when a high-ranking SS official visited.

Helga, like many of the others, spent much of her free time reading. Her favorite books were *Les Misérables* by Victor Hugo, an English edition of *Pollyanna*, and *The Gold Rush*, an exciting story about an American boy who ran away from home and traveled to the Yukon to look for gold.

Reading, like drawing, helped children forget where they were and took them to faraway places where there were no transports. The Nazis stocked a small community library with books written in German that they had stolen from Jewish homes. "People were literally starving for any kind of reading," recalled Dr. Emil Utitz, the professor in charge of the library. A group of teenagers even assembled a young people's library with an art exhibition.

Some children created their own reading materials. Kurt Jiří Kotouč and some of the other boys in Home One of L417 secretly published a magazine called *Vedem (In the Lead)*. Boys in another home, Q609, wrote a magazine called *Kamarád (Friend)*. They read these out loud every Friday night after work to welcome the Sabbath. The magazines contained their observations of and comments on life in the camp.

The SS did not want prisoners to know what was happening outside Terezin, and they did not want anyone from the outside to know what was going on inside the camp. They tightly controlled communication with the outside world.

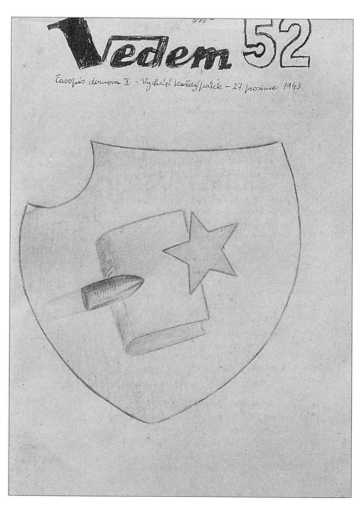

Title page of Vedem, *No. 52, December 27, 1943, pencil, crayons, pen, and brush. The symbol of* Vedem *was a spaceship and star, representing the future, and a book, which stood for learning.*

They censored the mail. There were no radios, newspapers, or magazines. But prisoners smuggled in radio parts. Men in the electrical workshop risked their lives by building a radio receiver and passing on news about the progress of the war.

Prisoners had coupons that entitled them to receive one package two or three times a year. Usually the packages contained food, clothes, and medicine sent by non-Jewish relatives and friends.

Friedl mailed her coupons to her friend Hilde and asked for special things to use in her work with the children. Once she asked Hilde to send her a book that she needed for a puppet show. Hilde refused because the Nazis had burned books by that author. Hilde knew that the SS searched packages. If they found the book, they might hurt Friedl. "Friedl was mad at us," remembered Hilde. "That was her—fascinated with an artistic idea, she wanted to put it into practice as soon as possible regardless of circumstances."

Building at Night *by Dita Polachová-Kraus (July 12, 1929–   ), charcoal. Dita Polachová-Kraus could see the Terezin church from her window in L410. She was fascinated by shapes, such as silhouettes of houses when the sun went down.*

Chapter 6
Fireflies

When Friedl packed for Terezin, she stuffed her
suitcase with dyed sheets. She planned to use
them as scenery and costumes for plays the children would perform. Friedl knew that children
loved acting, and she thought it would be good
for them to do group projects. At first it was
against the law to put on plays and give concerts.
Then the SS relaxed the rules. There were many
professional actors, directors, musicians, and university professors imprisoned at Terezin. Every
night the prisoners put on entertaining programs
for themselves—concerts, plays, poetry readings,
and lectures. On one November evening, for
instance, there were eleven different cultural
offerings to attend.

Friedl often gave lectures on teaching art to
children. She emphasized the importance of
allowing young children to freely express themselves. "Why are adults in such a hurry to make
children like themselves?" she wrote in her lec-
ture notes.

At Terezin in 1943, Friedl worked with other
tutors to help the children put on a production of
a Czech fairy tale called *Fireflies*. It was a musical
with dancing and singing. Under Friedl's direc-
tion, the children designed and made their own

Poster for Fireflies *by an unknown artist, watercolor. A poster
pinned on a bulletin board announced performances.*

I. KARPELES. HEIN B. 12.bl.

HANS KRÁSA
FLAŠINETÁŘ
Brundibár

DĚTSKÁ OPERA O 2 OBRAZECH

Hudebně nastudoval
A ŘÍDÍ: RUDOLF FREUDENFELD
Režie a scéna: Fr. Zelenka
TANEČNÍ SPOLUPRÁCE KAMILA ROSENBAUMOVÁ
Zpívají, hrají a tančí
DĚTI TEREZÍNSKÝCH DĚTSKÝCH ÚTULKŮ

Animals from *Brundibár by an unknown artist, pastel. Jerry Rind, a teenager imprisoned at Terezin, had a cousin who sang in Brundibár. He noted that the cat, dog, and sparrow in this picture represent characters from the opera.*

Poster for Brundibár *by an unknown artist, watercolor. Jerry Rind, who worked as a carpenter, pinched lumber intended for building bunks and coffins to make the fence used in a set.*

costumes. They used her dyed sheets and any scraps of material they could find or borrow—underwear, shirts, and even shrouds, which were used for wrapping corpses. Rehearsals and performances of *Fireflies* and other shows took place in dusty attics, dimly lit basements, and halls. Children and adults eagerly crowded in for performances. For an hour or two, actors and audiences forgot where they were. "We were in a dream world," recalled Ela Steinová-Weissberger.

Another favorite event was the children's opera *Brundibár*, composed by Hans Krása. Krása was a prisoner in Terezin and came to every performance. The story told of a brother and sister and their friends—a dog, cat, and sparrow—who outwit an evil organ grinder named Brundibár. "The final song, 'Brundibár Is Defeated, We Have Won,' had a special meaning

Photo of a performance of Brundibár *at Terezin. Ela Steinová-Weissberger (June 30, 1930–   ), who played the cat, is dressed in black and stands in the first row right directly in front of the conductor, Rudolf Fraňek (October 23, 1921–   ).*

Girls Dancing in a Meadow *by Anita Spitzová (January 6, 1933–October 4, 1944), pastel. In a contest that Friedl held, Anita Spitzová, who had never drawn anything before, won first place for a picture of girls dancing in a meadow.*

for us," recalled Ela, who had played the cat. Brundibár reminded everyone of Hitler, and when the children triumphed over him at the end of the opera, the audience cheered and

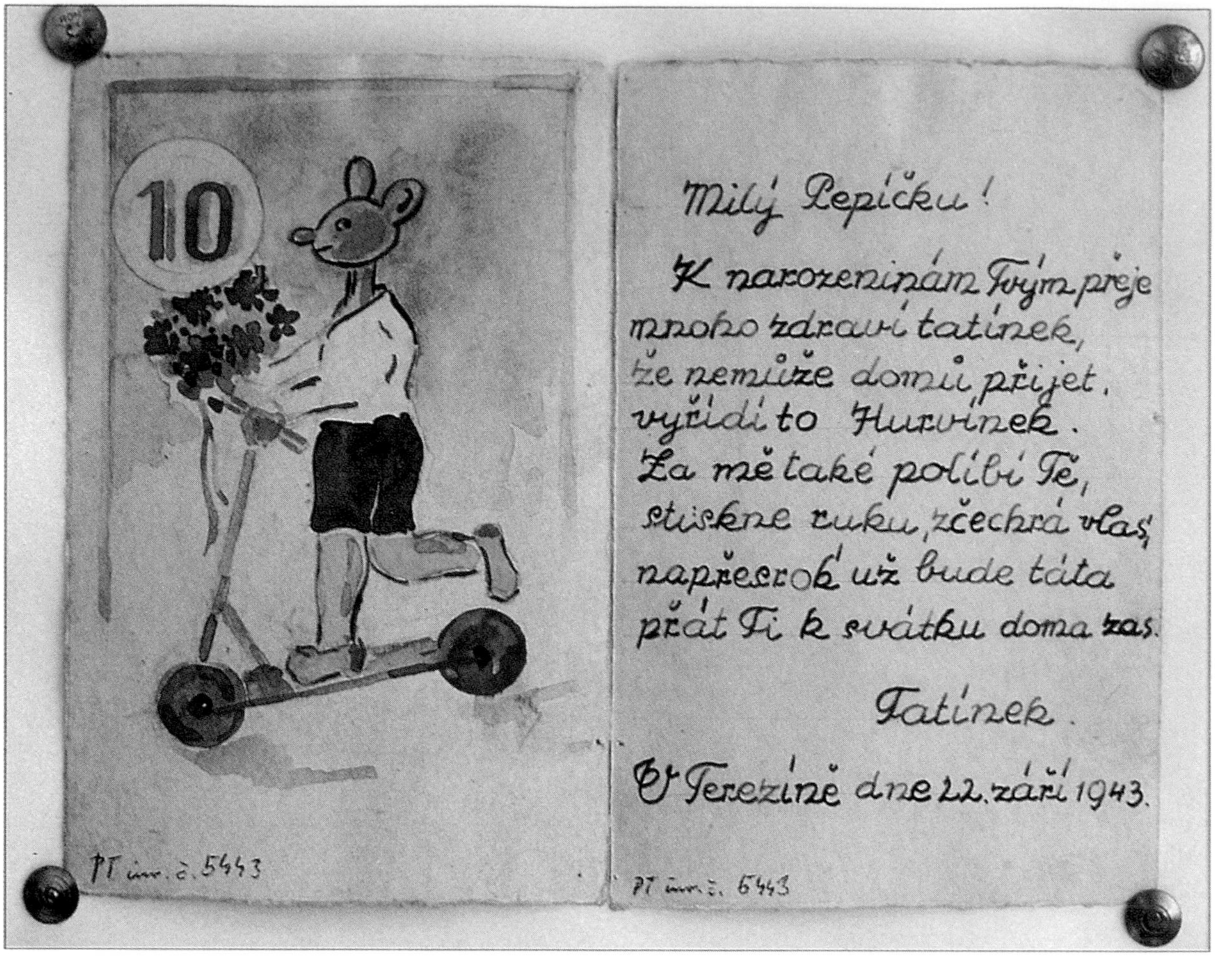

Milý Pepíčku!

K narozeninám Tvým přeje
mnoho zdraví tatínek,
že nemůže domů přijet.
vyřídí to Hurvínek.
Za mě také políbí Tě,
stiskne ruku, zčechrá vlas,
napřesrok už bude táta
přát Ti k svátku doma zas.

Tatínek.

V Terezíně dne 22. září 1943.

*Birthday card
painted by
Josef Bernard
for his son*

clapped. Friedl probably attended at least one of the fifty-five performances of *Brundibár*. The large cast included Dita Polachová-Kraus and many other students she knew well.

Friedl and her fellow tutors wanted the children to live as normal a life as possible at Terezin, despite the miserable conditions. Once Friedl held an exhibition of the children's artwork in the basement of L417. Seeing their drawings up on the wall made her students feel proud. It also gave them a chance to view and appreciate one another's work.

It was Friedl's birthday on July 30, 1944. Her students knew that she loved flowers, so they picked some for her while they were working in the fields and gardens of the SS. The girls smuggled the flowers into the camp under their blouses.

This picture by architect and stage designer František Zelenka (June 8, 1904–October 1944) was a thirteenth-birthday present for Eva Baierová (March 16, 1931–October 1944). Prisoners of all ages gave one another drawings and poems as birthday gifts.

Ten-year-old Erika Taussigová made her own gift. She drew a heart with flowers and wrote the words, "For Mrs. Brandeis."

Für Frau Brandeis *by Erika Taussigová (October 28, 1934–October 1944), pencil, 1944*

Chapter 7
Fooling the World

The Führer Gives the Jews a City
—Propaganda film, 1944

The Nazis did not want the world to know how horribly they were treating the Jews. They tried to deceive the world into thinking that Terezin was a wonderful place for Jews, a "paradise." Yet, despite their claims, some people did not believe them.

In April 1944, the International Red Cross demanded to have a visit to Terezin to see it for themselves. The Nazis prepared for the occasion by quickly beautifying the camp. Roses were planted in the town square. Buildings along the route where the visitors would walk were repainted. New buildings went up, including a concert bandstand in the square, a children's playground, a playing field for sports, coffee shops, and a community center. To make Terezin look less crowded, 7,500 prisoners, including many orphaned children, were shipped off to Auschwitz-Birkenau. Friedl and the other prisoners must have been horrified, yet they had to keep silent after the guests arrived.

On the day of the visit, June 23, SS officials escorted three representatives of the Red Cross on a carefully planned tour. The visitors never climbed a single flight of stairs to see what conditions were really like. The tour ended at the "community center," where children performed *Brundibár* and adults sang Verdi's *Requiem*. The Red Cross representatives were totally fooled. One of them, Maurice Rossel, a Swiss, said the ghetto was like "a normal town" and that the prisoners were treated well. Rossel wrote an enthusiastic report praising the "model ghetto" and the Nazis who ran it.

After the success of their hoax, the Nazis decided to make a propaganda movie about Terezin. They called it *Theresienstadt: A Jewish Settlement*. But the Jews gave it a sarcastic name: *The Führer Gives the Jews a City*. Using the sets they had put up just for the Red Cross visitors, the Nazis staged a glowing picture to "prove" they were treating their prisoners well. They chose the healthiest-looking adults and children to appear and ordered those who were sickly to stay out of sight.

Filming took place in August under the supervision of SS guards. Friedl refused to take part in the movie. She and most of the prisoners resisted the Nazis' scheme by staying away and not participating as extras. Phony scenes included smiling girls exercising outdoors, old people playing chess and chatting in a garden, little children riding rocking horses, and older kids eating thick slices of bread and butter—all things that happened only on the day of the filming. The grand finale was a performance of *Brundibár* in a real auditorium, with the audience of nicely dressed children sitting in regular seats.

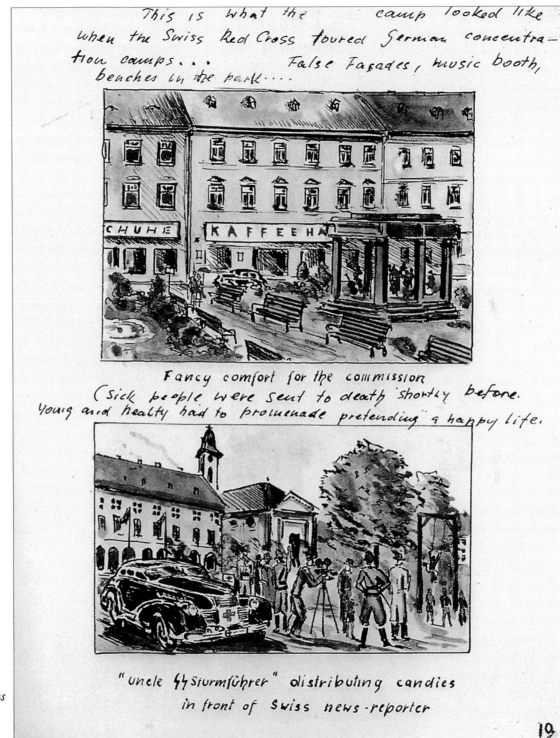

This is what the camp looked like when the Swiss Red Cross toured German concentration camps... False Facades, music booth, benches in the park....

Fancy comfort for the commission
(Sick people were sent to death shortly before. Young and healty had to promenade pretending a happy life.

"Uncle SS Sturmführer" distributing candies in front of Swiss news-reporter

19

Fancy comfort for the commission *and* "Uncle Sturmführer" *by Alfred Kantor (November 7, 1923–   ), watercolor, 1945. Alfred Kantor, an eighteen-year-old artist imprisoned first at Terezin, then at Auschwitz, made a book with pictures and captions of his experiences.*

Revealing actual conditions at Terezin was a crime punishable by death. Friedl's students and other children in the homes hid their drawings that showed true scenes of everyday life. Friedl stored such drawings in the attic.

Other professional artists imprisoned at Terezin worked in its graphics department, preparing maps, charts, and posters. But in their precious free time the artists courageously drew powerful pictures that told the truth about Terezin. They hid the drawings behind the walls and in the hollow panels of doors. They buried them in a tin box in a farmyard. One of the prisoners, František Strass, a former department store owner and art lover, bought the drawings for bread and sugar and smuggled them out to a dealer in Prague who sent them on to Switzerland. The SS found out. The artists were arrested and taken to SS headquarters for questioning.

The artists and their families and Strass and his wife were hauled off to prison in the Little Fortress. There they were tortured. Two died. Three were sent to Auschwitz.

Watercolor by Robert Bondy
(February 1, 1932–October 6, 1944)

Chapter 8
Telling the World

"Friedl left one transport before me to Auschwitz, and didn't return."

—Helga Polláková-Kinsky,
Terezin Diary, documentary

In autumn of 1944, the war was going poorly for the Nazis. They sharply increased the number of transports. On September 28, Friedl's husband, Pavel, was sent to Auschwitz on a transport of men only. He survived. Eight days later, on October 6, Friedl was sent to Auschwitz-Birkenau with thirty of her students. All perished.

The war ended in May 1945, when the Germans surrendered to the Allies. Russian soldiers freed prisoners still remaining at Terezin. Raja Englanderová-Žákníková, a teenage girl who had studied with Friedl, found five thousand of the children's drawings in two suitcases in the attic of L410. She gave the suitcases to Willi Groag, head tutor of L410. He was then in

Drawing of transport by an unknown artist in the magazine Kamarád, *pencil. In this drawing ghetto guards load prisoners onto freight cars.*

charge of finding good homes in Czechoslovakia and England where the children of Terezin, most of whom had become orphans, could recover. Willi brought the suitcases to Prague in August. They sat on a shelf for ten years until their contents were discovered and exhibited. Today the drawings, collages, and paintings are shown around the world. They belong to the State Jewish Museum in Prague and Beit Theresienstadt

Photographing prisoners at any of the death camps was strictly forbidden. But in May 1944 an unknown SS man took 185 pictures of prisoners arriving at Auschwitz-Birkenau, including this one. On April 11, 1945, Lili Jacob found an album of these pictures in a cupboard at a German labor camp called Dora 500 miles from Auschwitz-Birkenau. Lili, a prisoner, recognized people from her village whom she knew had been killed by the Nazis. In 1980 she gave the album to Yad Vashem.

in Israel, where they have been carefully cata-
logued and preserved.

In May 1947, the Czechoslovak government
established a Terezin memorial in the Little
Fortress, Terezin's prison. Survivors organized
the Terezin Association and founded the Ghetto
Museum in L417, the former home for boys.

Visitors now come to Terezin from all over
the world. Terezin exists as a memorial to the
courage and strength of those who did not sur-
vive, and to those who did. On display in the
museum are a selection of the children's drawings and one or two pieces by Friedl.

The very last drawing Friedl did was a delicate
watercolor of a young girl's face. She painted it
for Willi in an adult class to demonstrate how to
draw eyes. The girl's blue eyes are wide open.
She seems to gaze straight ahead, beyond
Terezin to the future. A future that Friedl
believed in for the children.

Friedl understood the power of art to sustain
hope. She lovingly enabled her students to rise
above their horrifying situation and find pleasure
and dignity through art. Their work is a lasting
testament to her influence. Those who knew her
never forgot Friedl Dicker-Brandeis.

Girl's Face *by Friedl Dicker-Brandeis, watercolor.*

Of the 15,000 children who passed through Terezin, only 100 survived. But their artwork and writings live on as testimony to their lives and spirits.

Gertruda Eisingerová (December 27, 1931–October 23, 1944) was ten years old when she arrived at Terezin. Many of her colorful drawings, such as the one below, were saved.

This is a list Friedl made of some of her students and their ages. No known survivors appear on it.

Ruth Schächterová (August 24, 1930–May 5, 1944) came to Terezin when she was twelve years old. She was a prolific artist. Her powerful collage depicting Terezin, above, is just one of many pieces of art she did as a student of Friedl's.

Ivo Leo Katz (April 11, 1932–July 1944) started out as a good-natured, cheerful, eleven-year-old boy. But the terrible conditions at Terezin made him angry and violent. When he drew with Friedl, he circled every shape with heavy black lines. A poem Ivo wrote began:

Some day we shall outrun this hour,
Some day there will be comfort for us,
And hope again burst into flower,
And peace and guardian care restore us.
The jug of tears will break and spill,
And death be ordered: "Hush, be still!"

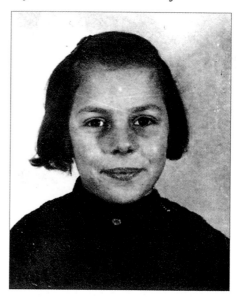

References

An asterisk (*) indicates works suitable for young readers.

Publications

*Auerbacher, Inge. *I Am A Star: Child of the Holocaust*. New York: Simon & Schuster, 1986.

Benešová, Miroslava, Vojtěch Blodig, and Marek Poloncarz. *The Small Fortress Terezin 1940–1945*. Translated from Czech by Petr Liebl. Terezin: The Terezin Memorial, 1996.

Berkley, George E. *Hitler's Gift: The Story of Theresienstadt*. Boston: Branden Books, 1993.

Blatter, Janet, and Sybil Milton. *Art of the Holocaust*. New York: The Rutledge Press, 1981.

Bondy, Ruth. *"Elder of the Jews": Jakob Edelstein of Theresienstadt*. New York: Grove Press, 1981.

Children's Drawings from the Concentration Camp of Terezin. Statni Zidovske Muzeum (Czech Republic). Prague, 1975.

Constanza, Mary S. *The Living Witness: Art in the Concentration Camps and Ghettos*. New York: The Free Press, A Division of Macmillan Publishing Co., Inc., 1982.

Dodwell, C. R., editor. *Jewish Art Treasures from Prague*. London: Lund Humphries in association with the Whitworth Art Gallery, University of Manchester, 1980.

Franz Singer–Friedl Dicker. Hochscule Für Angewandte Kunst in Wien, 1988–1989. (catalog) Fotos: Bauhaus Archive Berlin, Fritz Harand, 9 Dec. 1988 Bis 27 Jan. 1989.

Friedl Dicker-Brandeis, 1898–1944. Exhibition to commemorate the 90th anniversary of her birthday. The State Jewish Museum in Prague, 1988.

Glas-Larsson, Margareta. *I Want to Speak*. Riverside, CA: Ariadne Press, 1991.

Green, Gerald. *The Artists of Terezin*. New York: Hawthorn Books, Inc., 1969.

Greenfield, Hana. *Fragments of Memory*. Jerusalem: Gefen Publishing House Ltd., 1992.

*Holliday, Laurel, editor. *Children in the Holocaust and World War II: Their Secret Diaries*. New York: Washington Square Press/Pocket Books, 1995.

*Kantor, Alfred. *The Book of Alfred Kantor: An Artist's Journal of the Holocaust*. London: Piatkus Publishers, 1971.

Karas, Jŏza. *Music in Terezin 1941–1945*. New York: Beaufort Books Publishers in association with Pendragon Press, 1985.

Kramer, Edith. *Art as Therapy with Children*. Chicago: Magnolia Street Publishers, 1993.

———. *Childhood and Art Therapy*. Chicago: Magnolia Street Publishers, 1998.

Lederer, Zdenek. *Ghetto Theresienstadt*. New York: Howard Fertig, 1983.

*Makarova, Elena. *From Bauhaus to Terezin: Friedl Dicker-Brandeis and Her Pupils*. Jerusalem: Yad Vashem. The Holocaust Martyrs' and Heroes; Remembrance Authority, The Art Museum, 1990.

———. *Theresienstadt: Culture and Barbarism*. Stockholm, Sweden: Carlsson Bokforlag, 1995.

Redlich, Gonda. *The Terezin Diary of Gonda Redlich*. Saul S. Friedman, editor. Lexington: The University Press of Kentucky, 1992.

*Rogasky, Barbara. *Smoke and Ashes: The Story of the Holocaust*. New York: Holiday House, 1988.

Rubin, Judith Aron. *The Art of Art Therapy*. New York: Brunner/Mazel Inc., 1984.

Watercolor by Helga Polláková-Kinsky, (May 20, 1930–   )

Schwertfeger, Ruth. *Women of Theresienstadt: Voices from a Concentration Camp.* Oxford, England: Berg Publishers Limited, 1989.

Seeing Through "Paradise": Artists and the Terezin Concentration Camp. Boston: Massachusetts College of Art, 1991.

*Silten, R. Gabriele. *Between Two Worlds: Autobiography of a Child Survivor of the Holocaust.* Santa Barbara: Fithian Press, 1995.

Spies, Gerty. *My Years in Theresienstadt: How One Woman Survived the Holocaust.* Amherst, NY: Prometheus Books, 1997.

Terezin. Prague: Published by the Council of Jewish Communities in the Czech Lands, 1965.

Terezin in the Drawings of the Prisoners, 1941–1945. The State Jewish Museum in Prague, 1983.

Troller, Norbert. *Theresienstadt: Hitler's Gift to the Jews.* Translated by Susan E. Cernyak-Spatz; edited by Joel Shatzky. Chapel Hill and London: The University of North Carolina Press, 1991.

*Volavkova, Hana, editor. *I Have Not Seen a Butterfly Around Here: Children's Drawings and Poems from Terezin.* The Jewish Museum Prague, 1993.

*————. . . . *I Never Saw Another Butterfly . . . Children's Drawings and Poems from Terezin Concentration Camp 1942–1944.* Expanded Second Edition by the United States Holocaust Memorial Museum. New York: Schocken Books, 1993.

* *We Are Children Just the Same:* Vedem, *the Secret Magazine by the Boys of Terezin.* Prepared and selected by Marie Rut Krizkova, Kurt Jiři Kotouč, and Zdenek Ornest. Philadelphia and Jerusalem: The Jewish Publication Society, 1995.

*Weissova, Helga. *Draw What You See.* Edited by the Lower Saxony Society for the Preservation of Theresienstadt/Terezin. Göttingen: Wallstein Verlag, 1998.

Whitford, Frank. *Bauhaus.* London: Thames and Hudson, Ltd., 1984.

Videocassettes

* *Black & White is Full of Colours.* 1996. Tel-Aviv, Israel: A co-production of Argo Films and Czech TV in association with The New Foundation for Cinema and Television. Producer, Josef Platz. Producer, Alona Abt. Scriptwriter and director, Tamir Paul.

Echoes That Remain. Simon Wiesenthal Center Presents an Arnold Schwartzman Film, 1991. Written by Marvin Hier, produced by Arnold Schwartzman and Marvin Hier. Co-produced by Richard Trank. Los Angeles.

* *Edith Kramer: Artist/Art Therapist.* Sacramento: Chuck Connors Productions, 1994. Producer, Marilyn Halevi. Directors and videographers: Karen Waymire and Chuck Connors.

* *The Führer Gives a City to the Jews.* The National Center for Jewish Film, Brandeis University in Waltham, MA.

Genocide. Coproduced by Simon Wiesenthal Center. Written by Martin Gilbert and Marvin Hier. Produced by Arnold Schwartzman and Marvin Hier. Directed by Arnold Schwartzman. Los Angeles, 1981. 83 minutes.

* *Incarcerated Dreams.* uvadi, ABCD Video, 1992.

* *The Journey of Butterfly.* Bolthead Communications Group, Ltd. 1996. Directed by Robert E. Frye. 62 minutes.

The Music of Terezin. BBC Production in association with Czech Television, 1993.

* *Terezin Diary,* First Run/Icarus Films, 88 minutes/color. New York, 1990. A film by Dan Weissman and Zuzana Justman.

Theresienstadt 1941–1945. Theresienstadt Martyrs Remembrance Association, Kibbutz Givat Haim, Israel, 1988.

Theresienstadt: Gateway to Auschwitz. K.G.T. Film Corp., a Tomas Fantl Film, 58 minutes, 1988, Teaneck: Ergo Media Inc., An Elefantl Production, Jan Fantl, producer.

* *Voices of the Children.* Cinema Guild, 1996. Written and directed by Zuzana Justman. Produced by Jiri Jezek and Robert Kanter. A presentation of the Terezin Foundation, Inc.

Unpublished Diaries

* *Diary of Eva Ginzová.* Written in Terezin, July 1944–May 1945. Translated by Ivo Reznicek, March 1998.

The Diary of Helga Pollakova-Kinsky. Translated by Madeline Vadkerty, April 1998.

Diary of Mrs. Eva Noack-Mosse. Dr. Susan E. Cernyak-Spatz, 1995.

Diary of Petr Ginz. February 1944–September 1944. Translated by Ivo Reznicek, March 1998.

Helga Weissová's Diary (1939–1945). Translated by Dora Slaba.

Papers and Lectures

Cernyak-Spatz, Dr. Susan E. "Forgetting for the Future." 1995.

———. "Theresienstadt, A Threefold Paradigm of Deception." 1989.

———. "Hitler's Gift to the Jews." 1989.

———. "Theresienstadt, False Front and Heroic Reality." April 10, 1985.

Sound Recordings

Brundibár, A Children's Opera in Two Acts. Libretto by Adolf Hoffmeister, music by Hans Krása, and *Czech Songs*. Amsterdam, Holland, and Englewood, NJ: Channel Classics Records B.V., 1993.

Hebrew Requiem. Written by Eric Zeisl. London: The Decca Record Company, 1998.

Innocent Voices: The Verse of Terezin's Children. Composed and conducted by John Federico. Jefferson Valley, New York: Lost Planet Records, Inc., 1996.

The Song of Terezin. Written by Franz Waxman.

Terezin: The Music 1941–44 (Theresienstadt, Die Musik 1941–1944). OSA/MCPS/BIEM. London: Romantic Robot, 1991.

Volume 1: Chamber Music

1: Gideon Klein: Piano Sonata

2: Gideon Klein: Trio

3: Viktor Ullmann: String Quartet No. 3

4: Viktor Ullmann: Piano Sonata No. 6

5: Hans Krása: Dance

Volume 2: Vocal Works.

1. Hans Krása: Brundibár.

2. Viktor Ullmann: Four Songs for Mezzo-Soprano and Piano.

3. Pavel Haas: Four Songs on Chinese Verse.

CD

The Children's Homes in Ghetto Theresienstadt. 1941–1945. By Sharon Huppert. English edition by Dita Kraus. Theresienstadt Martyrs Remembrance Association, Beit Terezin, Givat Haim-Ihud, Israel.

Websites

(Beit Theresienstadt) Theresienstadt Martyrs Remembrance Association, http:www.ac.il/terezin

Jewish Museum in Prague, http:www.jewishmuseum.cz

Museum of Tolerance, motlc.wiesenthal.com

Simon Wiesenthal Center, www.wiesenthal.com

Terezin Memorial (Pamatnik Terezin), www.s.scr.cz/ascii/terezin/Index.html/

United States Holocaust Memorial Museum, www.ushmm.org

Yad Vashem, www.yad-vashem.org.il

House *by Erika Taussigová (October 28, 1934–October 16, 1944)*

Index

(Page numbers in italic type refer to illustrations)

Friedl Dicker-Brandeis (July 30, 1898–October, 1944)